Hazardous Waste Site Sampling Basics

Technical Note 414

BLM

December 2004
United States Department of the Interior • Bureau of Land Management

Technical Note 414

By:

Pamela S. Innis
Environmental Engineer
National Science and Technology Center
Denver, Colorado

Hazardous Waste Site Sampling Basics

Suggested citation:

Innis, Pamela S. 2004. Hazardous Waste Site Sampling Basics, Technical Note 414. Bureau of Land
Management, Denver, Colorado. BLM/ST/ST-04/001+1703. 35 pages.

Abstract

The Bureau of Land Management (BLM) is responsible for addressing releases of hazardous substances on public lands under their jurisdiction. This technical note provides technical guidance to those responsible for overseeing or conducting environmental sampling activities; provides information and references to assist field personnel in implementing technically consistent and responsive analytical sampling programs at hazardous waste sites; introduces the concepts and issues related to analytical sampling at hazardous waste sites; and provides a quick reference to websites and documents that can assist field personnel in implementing a site characterization plan.

Table of Contents

Figures and Tables

Introduction

The Bureau of Land Management (BLM) administers over 260 million acres of public lands. As part of its stewardship of these public lands, BLM is responsible for managing abandoned mine sites; illegal trespass/dump sites; abandoned facilities that used, stored, or disposed of hazardous substances; retired military areas; oil and gas production sites; and other potential hazardous waste sites. With this responsibility comes the necessity of characterizing the type of contaminants released at these sites. Sampling at hazardous waste sites is generally conducted to:

- Determine the immediate hazards to responders and the public
- Determine the short- and long-term risks to human and ecological receptors
- Determine if there is a need for an immediate (emergency) action or if an action is needed at all
- Determine the type of contaminants that have been introduced into the environment and the area that has been impacted by the release of the hazardous substance(s)
- Determine the Federal and State rules, regulations, and specific standards that will drive the need for cleaning up the site

- Determine the appropriate cleanup alternatives to mitigate current or potential threats

The field investigation that is selected for a site depends on the current level of knowledge about the site and the purpose of the sampling activities. Factors to consider when determining the methods for collecting and analyzing data are based on the quality of the data required. This document will not cover hazard categorization and field analytical methods. It should be recognized, however, that field analytical methods, such as the X-ray fluorescence spectrometer widely used within BLM for detection of elemental metals, are invaluable in supplementing laboratory analytical data during hazardous waste site characterization. This technical note will introduce the concepts and issues related to analytical sampling at hazardous waste sites and provide a quick reference to websites and documents that can assist field personnel in implementing a site characterization plan.

Further information concerning field analytical methods may be found in *Field Analytical and Site Characterization Technologies—Summary of Applications*, EPA-542-R-97-001, November 1997.

Existing Site Information

To adequately prepare for a field sampling effort, a review of existing site information is necessary. Site information can be obtained through sources such as past or present operators, government agencies, public citizens, databases, and libraries. The more informed the project team is prior to developing the sampling scheme, the more relevant the work plan will be.

Historical Research

The primary purpose of historical research is to complete a comprehensive review of available information concerning the site and to document evidence of the use, handling, and disposition of chemical products or waste materials, which may have caused a potentially adverse impact to the soil, surface water, or groundwater in the vicinity. Specifically, the intended result is to develop sufficient information from which a professional opinion can be made regarding the potential for a release of a hazardous substance into the environment and to identify areas requiring further investigation. Sources of historical data can include:

- Aerial photographs
- Preliminary assessments
- Phase I and II environmental site assessments
- Fire district records
- National Environmental Policy Act (NEPA) documentation, such as environmental assessments (EAs) and environmental impact statements (EISs)
- Newspaper articles
- Claim, permit, and lease information
- Historical U.S. Geological Survey (USGS) papers

- Maps
- State water resource or environmental agencies
- Environmental Protection Agency (EPA) Comprehensive Environmental Response, Compensation, and Liability Information System (CERCLIS) State list (http://www.epa.gov/superfund/sites/cursites)

Environmental Information

Significant information may be available regarding the geologic, hydrologic, biotic, and atmospheric conditions at or expected at the site. A search of the specific State environmental or water resources website may reveal databases that are available for the region in question. Some useful websites include:

- Stream gauging station data (http://waterdata.usgs.gov/nwis)
- Regional climate information (http://www.wrcc.dri.edu/index.html)
- Soil survey manuscripts (http://soils.usda.gov/survey)
- Well log records (State Water Resource Department websites)
- Local and regional geology (http://www.usgs.gov)
- Earth Resources Observation System (EROS) Data Center (http://edc.usgs.gov)
- National Oceanic and Atmospheric Administration (NOAA) (http://www.noaa.gov)

A field visit to the site is valuable in determining the sampling required. Information to obtain during the field survey should include the following:

- General site layout
- Property boundaries
- Site access requirements and restrictions

- General site conditions concerning surface water, soils, and air
- Potential receptors and contaminant migration pathways
- Visible sources of potential contamination
- Stressed vegetation
- Potential sources of offsite contamination

Data Quality Objectives

The Data Quality Objective (DQO) process is a planning approach that is used to prepare for sampling activities. The DQO process establishes specific objectives for an environmental study or sampling program and focuses data collection and analysis to meet those objectives. Appropriate use of the DQO process achieves two major objectives: it ensures that the type, quantity, and quality of data collected are appropriate for the decision at hand, and it eliminates the collection of unnecessary, redundant, and overly precise data.

The DQO process should be implemented early in the developmental stages of any project that requires data collection. It can apply to any size project, but the depth and detail of the process will vary depending upon the complexity of the project.

Key stakeholders should be involved with the DQO process. Stakeholders may include the project lead, contractors, State and Federal regulators, potentially responsible party (PRP) representatives, technical advisors, and managers.

The initial step in the DQO process is to define the questions, which should reveal the conditions and issues that must be resolved during the investigation (EPA 1994). Examples of this include:

- Is this a release as defined by section 101(22) of the Comprehensive Environmental Response, Compensation, and Liability Act (CERCLA)?
- Does the contaminant concentration exceed the State water quality criteria?

- Do the concentrations of metals exceed the Resource Conservation and Recovery Act (RCRA) hazardous waste criteria?
- Does the contaminant concentration exceed site background levels?

From these questions, the scope of the project can be defined and broken down into specific components that will define data collection constraints and methods. The components are basic and include:

- The physical boundaries of the site
- The source(s) of contamination
- The potential contaminants
- The characteristics of the contaminant (e.g., persistency, mobility, toxicity)
- The potential impacted media (e.g., air, surface water, groundwater, soil),
- Federal and State standards applicable to the site
- The impacts of the physical environmental system (e.g., geology, hydrology)
- The time frame in which the study will happen
- The potential receptors (targets)

It is necessary to define these components in order to proceed with the investigation. The stakeholders must agree on the definitions in order to eliminate unnecessary sampling and analysis, thereby reducing any reiterations during work plan development.

In addition to the decisions listed previously, other elements determined during the DQO process include the required detection level for the contaminants of concern and the probability and relevance of false positive and false negative errors in the analytical results.

A false positive error occurs when the hypothesis for a site is rejected when in fact it is true. For example, if a decision maker presumes that contaminant concentrations at a specified level indicate that there is no risk, a false positive error would occur when the decision maker determines, based on the sampling results, that there is still a risk remaining at the site when in fact there is not.

A false negative error would occur when the decision maker determines, based on the sampling results, that there is no risk when in fact there is a risk remaining.

Specifying limits on the probability of committing false positive and false negative errors reflect the decision maker's tolerable limits for making an incorrect decision. This will help determine the analytical methods to be applied in the work plan and the applicability of the various field screening methods. Stakeholders must also agree on the optimum number and location of samples.

For further information on the DQO process, the following EPA guidance is recommended: *EPA Guidance for the Data Quality Objectives Process*, EPA QA/G-4. EPA/600/R-96/055. September 1994.

Work Plan Development

Sampling and Analysis Work Plans document the decisions made during the DQO process. These plans must be developed before field activities are conducted. The two main components of a Sampling and Analysis Work Plan are the Field Sampling Plan (FSP) and the Quality Assurance Plan (QAP). The work plan may not specifically differentiate between the two, but it is important to recognize the significance of each and ensure that the elements described in the following two sections are included within the document. A checklist showing the key components is included as Figure 1.

Field Sampling Plan

The Field Sampling Plan is the portion of the work plan that describes how field personnel will actually perform the work. Specific elements of an FSP include:

Site description. As an introduction, a brief description of the site should be provided. Any relevant site history and pertinent site conditions that may affect the sampling should be discussed.

Location, number, and type of samples. A summary of the results of the DQO process should be provided in this section to give the rationale for the prescribed effort. An area map showing the site location and a refined map showing sample location detail should be included. If field screen methods are going to be used, detail should be included. Further information is provided in the Sample Design section of this technical note.

Work Plan Checklist

1. Field Sampling Plan

    a. Site Description .... ☐

    b. Location, Number, and Type of Samples .... ☐

    c. Sample Collection Methods .... ☐

    d. Equipment Decontamination Procedures .... ☐

    e. Record Keeping and Documentation Procedures .... ☐

    f. Laboratory Quality Assurance Plan (as an attachment) .... ☐

2. Quality Assurance Plan

    a. Technical Procedures for Sampling and Conducting Field Work .... ☐

    b. Quality Control Samples

        i. Field Samples .... ☐

        ii. Laboratory Samples .... ☐

    c. Corrective Action Plans .... ☐

    d. Chain-of-Custody Procedures .... ☐

    e. Instrument Calibration Procedures .... ☐

    f. Internal/External Inspection Reports .... ☐

    g. Personnel Qualifications/Training Records .... ☐

    h. Records/Logbooks .... ☐

    i. Analytical Reports/Data Packages .... ☐

    j. Data Verification/Validation Procedures .... ☐

Figure 1. Work Plan Checklist

Sample collection methods. A detailed description of the equipment, techniques, and procedures for collecting, labeling, preserving, packaging, and shipping samples should be provided. A field sampling summary table should be included for quick reference. The table should specify the number of samples per parameter per matrix, the preservatives, appropriate sample containers, and sample volumes. Table 1 provides an example of a method summary table.

Equipment decontamination procedures. An important part of any sampling effort is ensuring that field sampling equipment is properly cleaned and prepared. Failure to properly decontaminate equipment can introduce error into analyses through cross-contamination of samples. Laboratories can supply bottles and limited sampling equipment that are certified clean by the lab. This is a preferred option as the decontamination takes place in a controlled environment and it reduces the amount of investigation-derived waste.

The use of disposable or dedicated sampling equipment is also another consideration. In the event that field decontamination is necessary, a prescribed procedure for each type of sampling equipment should be provided. A typical procedure for hand-held sampling equipment is to remove gross contamination by rinsing with distilled water. A solution of anionic powdered detergent (e.g., Alconox) in distilled water is used to wash the equipment clean. If necessary, the use of brushes may be implemented to assist in removal of the material. The detergent wash is then followed by triple rinsing with distilled water. The final rinse is conducted with laboratory prepared deionized water. Clean equipment is then allowed to air dry and is placed in plastic bags for protection from further contamination.

Record keeping and documentation procedures. A discussion of the appropriate documentation for the project should be provided or referenced. The process for documenting changes to the approved sampling plan due to unforeseen field conditions should be detailed. Chain-of-custody and logbook documentation is further discussed in the next section.

Laboratory quality assurance plan. A copy of the analytical laboratory's internal quality assurance plan should be attached as an appendix to the FSP.

Quality Assurance Plan

The Quality Assurance Plan is the portion of the work plan that ensures sampling activities are performed with a high degree of confidence such that the resulting data will be representative of conditions found in the field. Specific elements of a QAP include:

Technical procedures for sampling and conducting field work. A complete description of the method-specific requirements for the samples should be provided. This should include sample bottle specifications, sample preservation requirements, sample shipping requirements, and holding times. Sample container labeling requirements should be identified. Container labels typically include the project name, date, and time of collection, specific analysis, preservative information, a unique sample identification number, and the sample initials or name.

Table 1. Method Specific Requirements

Method Specific Requirements

Method	Analyte Group	Bottle Required	Number of Bottles	Preservative	Holding Time	Laboratory
			WATER			
624	VOCs	40 ml amber vials	3	ascorbic acid, HCL	14 days	XYZ Analytical
625	SVOCs	1 liter amber glass	2	sodium sulfite, HCl	7 days	XYZ Analytical
608	PCBs and Pest	1 liter amber glass	2	sodium thiosulfate	7 days	XYZ Analytical
200.7/200.9	Metals	500 ml poly or glass	1	nitric acid	6 months	XYZ Analytical
245.1	Mercury	500 ml poly or glass	1	nitric acid	28 days	XYZ Analytical
200.8	Select Metals for SW	500 ml poly or glass	1	nitric acid	6 months	XYZ Analytical
SM3500 CRD	Hexavalent Chromium	500 ml poly or glass	1	none	24 hours	XYZ Analytical
300.0	Chloride	500 ml poly or glass	1	none	28 days	XYZ Analytical
300.0	Sulfate	500 ml poly or glass	1	none	28 days	XYZ Analytical
SM 4500S	Sulfide	500 ml poly or glass	1	NaOH + zinc acetate	7 days	XYZ Analytical
353.2	Nitrate/Nitrite	500 ml poly or glass	1	none	48 hours	XYZ Analytical
354.1	Nitrite	500 ml poly or glass	1	none	48 hours	XYZ Analytical
SM9221B	Fecal Coliform	100 ml bacti	1	sodium thiosulfate	6 hours	XYZ Analytical
405.1	BOD 5 day	1 liter HDPE	1	none	48 hours	XYZ Analytical
4500 NH3	Ammonia	500 ml poly or glass	1	sulfuric acid	28 days	XYZ Analytical
			SEDIMENT			
8260B	VOCs	16 oz glass	1	none	14 days	XYZ Analytical
8270B	SVOCs	16 oz glass	1	none	14 days	XYZ Analytical
8081A	Pest	16 oz glass	1	none	14 days	XYZ Analytical
8082	PCBs	16 oz glass	1	none	14 days	XYZ Analytical
6010A	Metals	16 oz glass	1	none	6 months	XYZ Analytical
7471A	Mercury	16 oz glass	1	none	6 months	XYZ Analytical
Carb 435	Asbestos	4 oz glass	1	none	none	XYZ Analytical

Quality Control Samples. Quality control samples ensure that the sampling methods produce representative samples of environmental media; confirm that laboratory analyses are reliable; verify that the quality of reported results is suitable to support decisions based on the environmental monitoring data; and provide a means to measure and document the uncertainty in analytical data. Specific quality control samples are discussed below.

Field Samples. A number of field quality control samples should be taken during waste site characterization. The stakeholders should agree to the specific quantity of quality control samples prior to the start of field activities.

- *Duplicate samples* are intended to identify variability in the analytical results associated with field and laboratory methods and the inherent heterogeneity of the media. Samples are taken at the same location employing the same collection methods.
- *Split samples* are used to identify variability between sampling handling methods or between laboratories. The sample material is homogenized in the field and placed into two separate sample containers for submittal to two separate labs.
- *Rinse blanks or equipment field blanks* analyses are used to assess the efficiency of equipment decontamination procedures in preventing cross-contamination between samples. The rinse blank will be analyzed for the same parameters as the investigative samples.
- *Trip blanks* provided by the laboratory will accompany the volatile organic samples collected each day in the field. The bottles should be sealed by the lab and are to remain closed until they reach the laboratory again. Trip blanks will

be analyzed for volatile organic compounds (VOCs) employing the same method used for the investigative sample and to help determine if contamination of the samples occurred enroute to the lab.

- *Temperature blanks* are containers of water that are shipped along with the samples enroute to the laboratory. The laboratory will measure the temperature of the blank upon receipt. This is used to verify that samples are maintained at less than 4 °C, which is necessary with many methods.

Laboratory Samples. The laboratory should include an internal quality assurance program. Laboratory reagent blanks (commonly called *method blanks*) are used to assess contamination during all stages of sample preparation and analysis. A laboratory fortified sample matrix (commonly called a *matrix spike*) should be used to evaluate the effect of the sample matrix on the recovery of the compound(s) of interest. One sample per batch should be split in the laboratory and analyzed in duplicate to provide an estimate of analytical precision. *Duplicate* analyses also are useful in assessing potential sample heterogeneity and matrix effects. An alternative to a sample duplicate is a *matrix spike duplicate*.

Corrective action plans. A discussion should be included within the QAP concerning corrective actions that will occur if a failure in the sampling/analysis process occurs. It should also identify who is responsible for implementing the corrective action. For example, if a senior reviewer determines in the review of field notes that a junior geologist incorrectly identified a soil horizon, additional training may be recommended and its completion should be documented in the site and personnel files.

Chain-of-custody procedures. The term "chain-of-custody" refers to the standard way of tracing the possession and handling of samples as they progress from the field to the analytical laboratory. It provides a record of when the samples were taken and through whose hands those samples passed along the way. A description of the procedures and requirements for sample custody, starting with sample collection through acceptance at the laboratory, should be provided. This should include methods for verifying sample container integrity, such as use of custody seals and chain-of-custody forms. The laboratory will supply chain-of-custody forms. Figure 2 provides a blank chain-of-custody form for reference.

Instrument calibration procedures. The QAP should identify the equipment used for performing data collection in the field. A description of or reference to the recommended calibration procedures and frequency of calibration for each field instrument should be provided. Methods for recordation of calibration for each instrument should be specified.

Internal/external inspection reports. Projects that require "critical" supplies should have acceptance criteria for the materials. A short description of the acceptance criteria for supplies and consumables from both internal and external sources should be provided. These criti-

cal items may include laboratory bottles, deionized water, reagents, calibration gases, and disposable equipment. The criteria could include provisions for certificates of cleanliness, testing, and purity. Acceptance would be based on the condition of the samples when received.

Personnel qualifications/training records. Any special training requirements or certifications required for personnel performing the specified tasks should be noted.

Records/logbooks. Each project should have a field logbook to accurately and completely document all field activities. Since field records are the basis for later written reports, language should be objective, factual, and free of personal feelings or other terminology that might prove inappropriate. Once completed, the field logbook becomes part of the project file. Information/observations to document within the field logbook include pertinent site descriptions, weather conditions, field data (e.g., pH, DO), including field equipment identification and calibration information, sample numbers and locations, sample descriptive information and relevant comments (e.g., odor, color, texture), client and supervisor instructions, visitor names and affiliations, and photo logs.

Analytical reports/data packages. A brief description of the data management procedures should be included or referenced. This includes data generated as part of the project, as well as data received from other sources.

LABORATORY NAME   CHAIN OF CUSTODY
LABORATORY ADDRESS

Report to:

Name: Address:

Company:

E-mail: Telephone:

Copy of report to:

Name: Address:

Company:

E-mail: Telephone:

Invoice to:

Name: Address:

Company:

E-mail: Telephone:

Project Information   **Analyses Requested**

Quote #:

Project/PO#:

Shipping Co.:

Tracking #:

Reporting State for compliance testing:

Sample Identification	Date/Time	Matrix	Number of Containers			

Matrix: SW (Surface Water) – GW (Groundwater) – DW (Drinking Water) – SL (Sludge) – OL (Oil) – Other (Specify)

Remarks

Relinquished by: Date/Time   Received by: Date/Time

Figure 2. Chain-of-Custody Form

Technical Note 414

Data verification/validation procedures. A description of the data verification/validation procedures should be provided. Criteria should be included for acceptance, rejection, or qualification of data based on elements including:

- Chain-of-custody records
- Laboratory quality assurance
- Compliance with sample handling, preservation, and analytical procedures

For further information on quality assurance, the following EPA guidance documents are recommended:

Quality Assurance/Quality Control Guidance for Removal Activities, Sampling QA/QC Plan and Data Validation Procedures. Interim Final. EPA/540/G-90/004. April 1990.

Guidance for Quality Assurance Project Plans, (QA/G-5), EPA/240/R-02/009. U.S. Environmental Protection Agency. Washington D.C., December 2002.

A BLM Instruction Bulletin is available that provides technical guidance for characterizing abandoned mine sites:

Information Bulletin No. RS-99-108 (07/14/99), Site Characterization for Abandoned Mine/Mill Sites can be found at: http://www.blm.gov/nhp/efoia/narsc/1999/IB/RSIB1999-108.pdf.

Sample Design

The design of the sampling plan is based on information gained during the development of the data quality objectives and on site-specific conditions. By carefully determining the sampling strategy, variability within the site can be determined and the data will be representative of actual site conditions. The location and frequency of sampling should be provided in detail within the sampling plan.

There are several sampling approaches that may be implemented at a site. The intent behind the selection of one sampling approach over another is to ensure that the sample reflects the characteristics of the population or media being sampled.

Biased/authoritative sampling involves the selection of locations based on knowledge of contaminant distribution and properties (such as homogeneity). Sample locations and quantities are based on the experience of the investigator. Rationale for sample selection must be well documented and defensible, particularly if the intent is to provide data in support of regulatory compliance. Biased sampling is often done if a population has obvious localized areas of high contamination to determine the "worst case" concentration of a contaminant(s). It is also used for screening purposes to determine if a release from a site has occurred. It must be understood that authoritative sampling will not accurately estimate the variance within the population or the extent of contamination and generally will not be acceptable to the regulatory community to demonstrate compliance.

Composite sampling consists of taking multiple samples over a temporal or spatial range, physically combining equal portions (or aliquots), and drawing one or more subsamples for analysis. It can provide improved precision in the sampling effort, while reducing the required number of samples. Composite samples are taken primarily when an average concentration is sought and there is no need to detect peak concentrations. Composite samples are most valuable in large study areas with sampling grids that cover areas from 100 to 500 feet per side. It must be understood, however, that the integrity of volatile organic compounds (VOCs) will likely be compromised during the mixing of the sample. Composite samples for VOCs are generally not recommended for soil matrices.

Grab samples are samples taken from a particular location at a distinct point in time. They are valuable when a biased sample location is selected, particularly when determining "hot spots" or background.

Unbiased/random sampling is based on mathematical and statistical theories. Random sampling is typically applied to waste sites with unknown or variable concentrations.

Technical Note 414

For further information on composite sampling, a detailed discussion is provided in the *Standard Guide for Composite Sampling and Field Subsampling for Environmental Waste Management Activities* (ASTM 6051-96).

The sample locations are determined through the development of a sample unit grid for the site. The area of each unit within the grid is based on the area of the site and the quantity of samples determined within the DQO process.

There are three basic patterns for selection of random sampling locations: simple, stratified, and systematic.

Simple—In simple random sampling, all potential sample locations in a waste unit are identified and given a number. A suitable number of sample locations are selected through the use of a random number generator. Each unit in the population is selected with equal probability. The investigator should make an estimate in the potential variability of the population. A more heterogeneous unit would likely require more sampling locations.

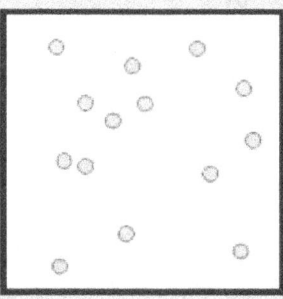

Stratified— Environmental media or populations may be separated temporally or spatially and have properties that are different from an adjacent portion. In stratified sampling, areas of non-uniform properties or concentrations are identified and

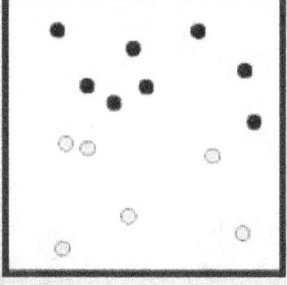

segregated. For example, a waste site may be stratified based on particle size or color. Simple random samples are collected from each stratum. The number of samples per stratum can be based on factors such as size of the strata, accessibility to the strata, or apparent variability within the strata.

Systematic—In systematic sampling, the first sampling point is randomly selected and all subsequent sample locations are at fixed intervals from that point. This method is often preferred as it is easy to implement in the field and contamination patterns are more readily identified. To improve on the randomness of the sampling design, the sample location within the individual grid unit can be varied.

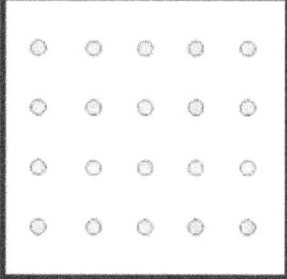

Background samples are samples collected at or near the waste site in areas not influenced by site contamination. It demonstrates the ambient concentrations of a substance from both naturally occurring and anthropogenic non-site sources. Background samples are collected from each media of concern: soil, sediment, surface water, groundwater, and air. The sample locations should have the same basic characteristics as the medium at the site. The number of background samples is site specific and dependent on the media sampled, the type of contaminant, and the availability of background sample locations. The number of samples should, however, be sufficient enough to reduce or eliminate the potential determination that concentrations of a constituent at the site are higher than background when in they in fact fall within the range. It should be understood that a difference in the concentration of background samples and site samples should not, in itself, trigger a cleanup action at the site. It indicates that further evaluation of the data must be completed.

For further information, several references are available through EPA that will assist in the development of the sampling plan for the site. Other references on environmental sampling can be requested from the BLM Library.

Subsurface Characterization and Monitoring Techniques: Desk Reference Guide, Volumes 1 and 2. EPA/625/R-93/003 a, b. May 1993.

Abandoned Mine Site Characterization and Cleanup Handbook. EPA530-C-01-001. March 2001.

Site Characterization for Subsurface Remediation. EPA/625/4-91/026. November 1991.

RCRA Waste Sampling Draft Technical Guidance – Planning, Implementation and Assessment. EPA530-D-02-002, August 2002.

Sampling Considerations and Techniques

The proper selection of a sampling methodology must be done to ensure that the samples will be representative of the site. The methods are matrix dependent. In some situations, there may be several options to consider. For others, the analyte or site conditions may dictate a specific sampling method. A list of sample collection methods is provided in Table 2, Field Sampling and Collection Techniques.

One issue to consider when sampling for a variety of analytes is the composition of the equipment used in the sampling. Equipment composed of the same material as the analyte that is being sampled for may influence the data. Consideration should be given to using glass, Teflon, or stainless steel sampling equipment when analyzing for trace organic compounds, and to using Teflon, plastic, or glass equipment when sampling for trace metals.

Soil

The selection of soil sampling equipment is based on site-specific conditions and the nature of the contaminant of concern. For example, the sensitive nature of volatile organic compounds (VOCs) requires special consideration. Equipment that disrupts the sample material may cause a release of volatiles into the ambient air. The optimum sample collection device will allow field personnel to collect minimally disturbed samples and will enable them to provide an accurate field description or log of the lithology.

Another consideration in the sampling of soils is the homogeneity or heterogeneity of the media. Many contaminants, particularly organics and radionuclides, bond differently to different soil types or particle sizes. In a heterogeneous sample area, there may be considerable variability in contaminant concentrations. Additionally, in media with large disparity in the size fraction, the tendency may be to collect the smaller fraction. This may introduce error in the overall concentration of the media. These situations should be well documented and considered in the analysis of the data.

Sediment

Sediment sampling in surface water offers many challenging aspects. Suspended particles are carried in surface water until turbulent intensity no longer exceeds particle fall velocity. If a contaminated media is introduced, intermixed layers of native material and waste material will characterize the stream bottom. These layers may or may not be consistently located. During times of variable flow, the areas of ebbing flow may change and solids may be resuspended.

One must evaluate the capability of sampling equipment to extract a representative sample from a saturated environment. Capturing the finer material, when collecting a sample, is difficult in that it may be carried away with outflowing water from the sampler.

Table 2. Field Sampling and Collection Techniques

Technique	Analyte	Soil	Sludge	Sediment	Surface Water	Ground Water	Soil Gas/ Air	Drums/ Containers	Biota	IDW Volume	Depth	Comments
Drilling Methods												
Hollow Stem Auger	1–11	+	-	+	-	-	-	-	-	High	100'	Not applicable to consolidated formations. Soil sample is a disturbed sample. Difficult drilling in saturated soils or soils with cobbles.
Mud Rotary	1–11	+	-	+	-	-	-	-	-	High	1000'	Potential loss of drilling fluids in fractured or unconsolidated formations. Not recommended for drilling in contaminated zones due to IDW generation.
Air Rotary	2, 4–11	+	-	+	-	-	-	-	-	Med	>1000'	Cuttings may present a contamination/health hazard. Hydrocarbons used during drilling may contaminate samples.
Sonic	1–11	+	-	+	-	-	-	-	-	Low	<500'	Method may be more expensive than others. Continuous core useful in lithologic description.
Cable Tool	2, 4–11	+	-	+	-	-	-	-	-	High	<5000'	Minimum size casing is 4 inches. VOC samples may be compromised. Hard tooling compromises lithologic description.
Diamond Drilling	2, 4–11	+	-	+	-	-	-	-	-	Med	>1000'	Primarily used in consolidated formations. Solid core useful in detection of fracture zones and lithologic changes.
Drive Methods and Other Methods												
Cone Penetrometer	1–11	-	-	-	-	+	+	-	-	Low	<100'	Not applicable in consolidated formations.
Direct Push Sampler	1–11	-	-	-	-	+	+	-	-	Low	<100'	Not applicable in consolidated formations.
Backhoe	1–14	+	+	+	-	-	-	-	+	High	25'	Personnel cannot enter pits deeper than 3 feet without shoring and confined space training. Exposure to and spread of contamination increased. Prior knowledge of subsurface conditions useful.
Liquid/Water Collection Methods												
Bladder Pump	1–12	-	-	-	+	+	-	+	+	Med	100' +	Bladder may break. Large volumes of compressed gas required for deep or prolonged sampling.
Inertia Pump	1–11	-	-	-	+	+	-	+	-	Med	<100'	Difficult to operate in larger/deeper wells. Manually intensive operation.
Bailer	1–12	-	-	-	+	+	-	+	+	High	200'	Difficult for deeper wells. Volatiles may be lost. Limited in volume collected at one time. Depth specific samples difficult to obtain.

Table 2. Field Sampling and Collection Techniques (continued)

Technique	Analyte	Soil	Sludge	Sediment	Surface Water	Ground Water	Soil Gas/ Air	Drums/ Containers	Biota	IDW Volume	Depth	Comments
Submersible Pump	1–11	-	-	-	+	+	-	+	-	Med	<100'	Chemistry altered at high pumping rates. Flow rate cannot be controlled.
Peristaltic Pump	1–12	-	-	-	+	+	-	+	+	Med	25'	Low pumping rates make purging wells difficult. Volatiles may be lost.
Gear-driven Pump	1–11	-	-	-	+	+	-	+	-	Med	<100'	Constant flow rate (not variable). High suspended solids cause gear wear.
Gas-Driven Displacement Pump	1–11	-	-	-	+	+	-	+	-	Med	<100'	Dedicated pump for wells.
Diffusive Bag Sampler	1,3	-	-	-	+	+	-	-	-	Low	200'	
COLIWASA	1–11	-	+	-	+	-	-	+	-	Low	-	Typically used for containerized waste. Difficulty in sampling highly viscous liquids.
Weighted-Bottle Sampler	1–11	-	-	-	+	+	-	-	-	Low	100'	Can collect depth specific samples. Compatibility of liquid with sampler construction material must be verified.
Kemerer/Van Dorn Depth Specific Sampler	1–11	-	-	-	+	+	-	+	+	Low	200'	Difficult to operate at depth. Cross-contamination may occur as sampler is lowered to desired depth. Activating mechanism prone to malfunction and damage.
Pneumatic Depth Specific Samplers	1–11	-	-	-	+	+	-	-	-	Low	200'	Large volume sample requirements difficult to acquire.
Bacon Bomb Sampler	1–11	-	-	-	+	+	-	+	-	Low	100'	Suspended solids may cause problems with seal. May aerate sample, compromising VOCs. Brass construction incompatible with some liquids.
Stratified Sample Thief	1–11	-	+	-	-	-	-	+	-	Low	-	Typically used for containerized waste. Plastic construction material may not be compatible with some substances.
Depth Integrating Sampler	1–11	-	-	-	+	-	-	-	-			Typically used to obtain a discharge-weighted sample along the stream cross section
Hand-Held Methods												
Scoop/Spoons/ Shovels	1–14	+	+	+	-	-	-	-	+	Low	Near Surface	VOCs may be compromised
Hand Auger	1–14	+	+	+	-	-	-	-	+	Med	<10'	VOCs may be compromised. Lithology identification difficult.
Drive Tubes	1–14	+	+	+	-	-	-	-	+	Low	<15'	Sample may be lost in wet conditions. Sample collection difficult in large gravels and cobbles.

Table 2. Field Sampling and Collection Techniques (continued)

Technique	Analyte	Soil	Sludge	Sediment	Surface Water	Ground Water	Soil Gas/Air	Drums/Containers	Biota	IDW Volume	Depth	Comments
Encore Sampler	1–6	+	+	+	-	-	-	-	-	Low	Surface	Used for subcoring samples for collection of VOCs and SVOCs.
Bottle/Bucket Grab Samples	1–14	+	+	+	+	-	-	+	+	Low	Surface	
Grain Sampler	1–11	+	-	-	-	-	-	+	-	Low	5'	Useful for sampling granular or powdered material.
Gas/Air Collection Methods												
Soil Gas Probe	1,3	+	-	-	-	-	+	-	-	Low	100'	Results dependent on soil matrix conditions. Probes may clog but can be cleared with wire.
Mylar/Teflon/Tedlar Bag	1–9	-	-	-	-	-	+	-	-	Low	-	Moisture may affect results. Pumps used in combination. Bag selection based on resistance to adsorption and permeation of contaminant of concern.
Canister	1–9	-	-	-	-	-	+	-	-	Low	-	Moisture may affect results.
Passive Soil Gas Sampler	1,3	+	-	-	-	-	+	-	-	Low	25'	Vertical profile use is limited. Concentrations area barometrically dependent and averaged over time.
Constant Flow Sampler	1–9	-	-	-	-	-	+	-	-	Low	-	Type of pump is dependent on physical properties of the contaminant, the collection medium, and the flow rates required for the specified method.
Vacuum Pump Sampler	1–9	-	-	-	-	-	+	-	-	Low	-	Moisture may affect results.
Passive Air Sampler	1–9	-	-	-	-	-	+	-	-	Low	-	Used for collection of samples for dispersed liquids (mists and fogs) and solids (dust, fumes, smoke).
Particulate Samplers and Cassettes	1–9 and PM$_{10}$	-	-	-	-	-	+	-	-	Low	-	
Impingers/Bubblers	1–9	-	-	-	-	-	+	-	-	Low	-	
Biota Sampling Methods												
Electrofishing	1–11, 15	-	-	-	-	-	-	-	+	Low	-	Useful in areas with uneven bottoms. Downstream collection may be necessary.
Snorkeling/Angling	1–11, 15	-	-	-	-	-	-	-	+	Low		Nets can become clogged. Towing speeds should be low when using nets to avoid diversion effects.
Nets	1–12, 14,15	-	-	-	-	-	-	-	+	Low		
Dredge/Grab Sampler	2, 4–14	-	+	+	-	-	-	-	+	High		Descent of tool may disturb fines. Possible loss of material when pulling sample. Jaws may become lodged open.

Modified from Naval Facilities Engineering Command and the U.S. Environmental Protection Agency, 1998, *Field Sampling and Analysis Technologies Matrix and Reference Guide* (Appendix D), First Edition.

Table 2. Field Sampling and Collection Techniques (continued)

LEGEND

+ Applicable technology
- Not an applicable technology

Analytes/Biota Type

1. Non-halogenated volatile organics
2. Non-halogenated semi-volatile organics
3. Halogenated volatile organics
4. Halogenated semi-volatile organics
5. Polynuclear aromatic hydrocarbons
6. Pesticides/herbicides
7. Metals
8. Radionuclides
9. Other inorganics (asbestos, cyanide, fluorine)
10. Explosives
11. Total Petroleum hydrocarbons
12. Plankton
13. Bacteria and other periphyton
14. Benthos
15. Fish

Depth Limitations

The limitations sited are maximum depth in ideal conditions.
Site-specific conditions may reduce the efficiency of the method.

Surface Water

Surface water environments encountered on BLM land can generally be put into three groupings: rivers, streams, and creeks; lakes and ponds; and surface impoundments and lagoons. The type of sample collection technique must be adapted to the specific conditions of the water body. Conditions to consider include flow, depth, turbulence, and vertical stratification due to temperature gradients. In rivers, streams, and creeks, samples should be collected immediately downstream of turbulent areas or downstream of any marked physical change in the channel to ensure representativeness (EPA 1996). Care should be taken to minimize the disturbance of sediment when taking samples. Sampling of lakes, ponds, impoundments, and lagoons is dependent on the size of the basin as well as the number of tributaries. Vertical composites along a cross-section of larger water bodies should provide adequate coverage of the area. In small water bodies, one composite sample may be considered sufficient. Vertical composites should not, however, be taken for VOCs. For this analysis, separate grab samples should be taken.

The USGS *National Field Manual for the Collection of Water-Quality Data* is a thorough document that covers both surface water and groundwater sampling. It is targeted "specifically toward field personnel in order to (1) establish and communicate scientifically sound methods and procedures, (2) provide methods that minimize data bias and, when properly applied, result in data that are reproducible within acceptable limits of variability, (3) encourage consistent use of field methods for the purpose of producing nationally comparable data, and (4) provide citable documentation for USGS water-quality data-collection protocols. It informs field personnel of the major steps needed to prepare for water-quality data-collection activities, select surface-water sampling sites, make reconnaissance visits to ground-water sampling sites and select wells that will meet scientific objectives, and set up electronic and paper files." The manual can be found at: http://water.usgs.gov/owq/FieldManual.

Groundwater

When sampling groundwater, prior knowledge of the well conditions and construction is necessary. This includes identification of the lithology of the area. Information can be gained by reviewing drilling logs and previous sampling records. Variations in well construction and lithology will help determine the amount of water that must be purged from the well. The purpose of well purging is to remove stagnant water in the wellbore and adjacent sand pack in order to get a sample that is representative of the surrounding formation.

Selection of the well sampling device will depend on many factors, such as depth of the well, diameter of the well, and yield of the formation. In some instances, it may be appropriate to implement depth-specific sampling. If the contaminant of interest is a VOC, care must be taken in selecting a method to assure that aeration/degassing of the water does not occur.

Further information on sediment and surface water sampling can be found in Chapter A8 of the USGS National Field Manual for the Collection of Water-Quality Data at: http://water.usgs.gov/owq/FieldManual/Chapter8/index.html.

Air

Air monitoring is done at a hazardous waste site for two purposes: to monitor the potential exposure to onsite workers, and to monitor the potential exposure to surrounding populations. The significant difference in monitoring the two is that potential exposure at the workplace occurs for approximately 8 hours, 5 days a week, whereas potential exposure to surrounding populations is continuous throughout the week. The monitoring program must reflect this difference.

Air monitoring methodologies can be divided into several categories. In general, monitoring is done at either a fixed station or via personal air monitors. Fixed or stationary station monitors are often located at the boundaries of a waste site to measure the potential migration of a contaminant off the site. This method is often implemented continuously during cleanup activities. Personal air monitors are used primarily for workers during the time they are in the contaminated area.

Air monitoring can be further subdivided into active or passive methods. *Active methods* employ the use of pumps or vacuum devices, whereby the air sample is mechanically entrained within a specified media or contained in a bag or canister that will be submitted for analysis. The sorbent media used is specific to the contaminant of interest. A flow meter or valve is used to ensure that air is collected at a constant rate over a specified period of time. *Passive methods* either require air movement across the device or simple diffusion or permeation of a compound to equilibrium with the surrounding conditions.

Drums or Containerized Waste

Health and safety is paramount when sampling drums or containerized waste and should be performed by experienced hazardous waste technicians. Old, deformed, or bulging containers indicate a potentially unstable situation. Attempts should not be made to sample drums and containers until the internal pressure is at equilibrium with the atmospheric pressure. The conditions of a drum may also dictate overpacking prior to sampling. Air monitoring should occur during sampling of drummed or containerized waste.

In situations where numerous containers are present, verifiable information may be used to reduce the number of containers that are sampled. If such information is not available, each container should have a discrete sample.

Sampling of containerized solids is done via a grab sample or a composite sample, depending on the size of the container and the sampling objective.

When sampling containerized liquids, the potential for layering exists. The use of sampling devices that take this potential into account is recommended. The stratified sample thief or Composite Liquid Waste Sampler (COLIWASA) are designed to address layering of liquids. Depending on the objective of the sampling event, a composite of the liquid may be desired or a discrete sample of each layer may be preferred.

Waste Piles

Waste piles are frequently encountered on abandoned mine lands and processing facilities. When determining the sampling protocol to be employed for waste piles, several factors must be considered.

Initially, the volume of the waste pile should be determined. State or Federal regulations may require a certain number of samples per unit volume. Unless significant background information is available regarding the processing used at the site, waste piles should be considered heterogeneous. Exposure to the elements may also cause variability within a waste pile. The sampling strategy should take into account vertical and lateral changes.

Several sampling methods may need to be implemented to adequately characterize waste piles. As with soils, site-specific or contaminant-specific conditions may dictate the selected methodology.

Sludges and Slurries

Sludges and slurries are a mixture of solids and liquids. Generally, sludge consists of more solids or a more viscous liquid such as crude oil. When sampling sludges and slurries, it is necessary to ascertain whether the material is layered. This is particularly true of surface impoundments. Larger surface impoundments may require grab samples at several locations and depths, whereas drums and small pits may call for only one sample.

When sampling sludges and slurries, the nature of the material will dictate the type of sampling equipment. The more solid materials can be sampled with soil or sediment sampling equipment, while liquid samplers may be more appropriate for some slurries. It is prudent to consider disposable equipment when sampling the more viscous sludges.

Biota

Indigenous species can be used as an indicator of the biological effects of pollutants more accurately than predictions from chemical analyses. The effects of contaminants can occur directly or through bioaccumulation. For instance, examining the biodiversity of a river or stream can provide insight into the overall health of that environment. The larvae of mayflies, caddisflies, stoneflies, and true flies have been used to identify point sources of environmental hazards in streams and other wetlands. It is important to clearly define the objective of biota sampling in the DQO process.

Biological data are highly variable. Information gained from biota sampling is more valuable if there is a direct correlation, both spatially and chronologically, to sampling of other media. Sample locations should be as near as possible to soil, sediment, or surface water sample locations. The analysis of the information from the sampling will require a multidisciplined individual or team of individuals.

Artificial substrates may be considered for sampling periphyton and benthos in aquatic environments. These substrates may result in a more representative sampling as variation induced through direct sampling are lowered and the method is relatively straightforward.

When taking plant samples, the entire plant should be collected if size and conditions allow. If this is not possible, field personnel should emphasize collection of complete leaves, reproductive structures, and stem sections. Sample size, preservation, and storage criteria depend on the material sampled, the environment of origin, and the requested analysis.

The recordation of field observations during the collection of biota is important. Field personnel should note any variation in conditions that exist in the potentially contaminated area compared to the surrounding area. Theses variations include the existence of plants that appear stressed, reduced or eliminated species populations, or any other conditions that could be considered abnormal.

Soil Gas Surveys

Soil gas surveys are used for detection of VOCs in the area between the surface and groundwater known as the vadose zone. They are used to help delineate the boundaries of a contaminant plume both in the groundwater and vadose zone and are useful in finding potential sources.

As with ambient air monitoring, soil gas monitoring methods employ the use of *active methods* and *passive methods*. The use of pumps or vacuum devices is applied when pipe probes or gas piezometers are installed. The sample is then collected in a contaminant- specific media, a bag, or a canister. *Passive methods* utilize simple diffusion or permeation of a compound into a sorbent material until equilibrium with the surrounding conditions is achieved.

For current information on emerging technologies, consult the Field Analytical Technologies Encyclopedia (FATE) website, developed jointly by EPA and the Army Corp of Engineers, which provides up-to-date information about characterization technologies. This can be found at http://FATE.CLU-IN.ORG.

Analytical Methods

The selection of the analytical method for the waste stream or media depends on several factors. Many of these factors will be determined in the Data Quality Objective (DQO) process. Available information regarding the site and the known or potential contaminants will help guide the method selection.

In considering contaminants that have more than one analytical method, it is valuable to examine the method detection limits (MDL). The Code of Federal Regulations (40 CFR Part 136) provides the definition of MDL as "the minimum concentration of a substance that can be measured and reported with 99 percent confidence that the analyte concentration is greater than zero and is determined from analysis of a sample in a given matrix containing the analyte." Some methods may not achieve the level required by regulatory levels or necessary for risk analysis. There are situations where enforceable water quality limits are below the MDL. Early communication with the regulatory community is advisable in these instances. Communication with the selected laboratory is also important. The methods implemented at laboratories vary. If lower detection limits are required for certain analytes, the use of several labs may be necessary.

The nature of the material being sampled may also dictate the analytical method to be used. Methods that apply specifically to drinking water standards may not directly apply to the water being sampled at the site. When sampling to determine if a waste is regulated as a Resource Conservation and Recovery Act (RCRA) toxicity characteristic waste, the method to be implemented is the Toxicity Characteristic Leaching Procedure or TCLP.

Sample Preservation

Sample preservation is done to minimize any changes, either physical or chemical, that may occur between sample collection and laboratory analysis. Without preservation, sample concentrations may not be representative of the actual conditions at the site.

The EPA publication SW-846, *Test Methods for Evaluating Solid Waste, Physical/Chemical Methods,* is the Office of Solid Waste's official compendium of analytical and sampling methods that have been evaluated and approved for use in complying with the RCRA regulations. SW-846 functions primarily as a guidance document setting forth acceptable, although not required, methods for the regulated and regulatory communities to use in responding to RCRA-related sampling and analysis requirements. Online access to the test methods is available through the EPA at http://www.epa.gov/epaoswer/hazwaste/test/main.htm.

The appropriate method of preservation is dependent on the physical characteristics of the sample, the concentration of the analytes in the sample, and the analytical method. You should consult with the laboratory concerning the addition of chemical preservatives. Many laboratories will supply preservatives for the specific sample. The preservatives may be premeasured and placed in the sample containers or a separate preservative may be supplied for addition to the sample bottle.

Holding Times

Sample concentrations can degrade over time. To minimize this, the specific analytical methods have designated holding times. Samples that are analyzed outside of their specified holding times are considered qualified and can only be used to demonstrate whether a concentration exceeds a regulatory threshold, such as water quality criteria or hazardous waste designation levels. They cannot be used to demonstrate compliance.

Work Plan Implementation

Once the work plan is developed, additional support activities are necessary prior to actual sampling plan implementation. These activities include:

- Ensuring site access
- Procurement of subcontracts (e.g., drilling contractor, analytical laboratory)
- Coordinating shipment of sample containers and chain-of-custody forms from the laboratory
- Procurement of field equipment (personal protective equipment or PPE, sampling equipment)
- Calibration of field monitoring equipment

Prior to performing any field sampling, a site Health and Safety Plan (HASP) must be developed. The HASP shall comply with the Office of Safety and Health Administration (OSHA) standards for hazardous waste site operations (40 CFR §1920.120) and shall specifically address the following: health and safety policies, key personnel health and safety responsibilities, employee responsibilities, PPE, standard work practices, medical monitoring, exposure monitoring, health and safety program documentation, and the personnel training program.

As the information about the current conditions of the site may be limited, flexibility in the field may be required. It should be expected that the number and location of samples specified in the work plan might need to be modified based on changes in the field. Documentation of all field changes should be completed.

Technical Note 414

A recommended reference for use in the field is *Description and Sampling of Contaminated Soils: A Field Pocket Guide* (EPA/625/12-91/002, November 1991). The guide provides procedures and site characterization information that is valuable when performing reconnaissance or a detailed investigation of a site.

Additional Information and Technical Support

As stated earlier, the purpose of this technical note is to introduce the concepts and issues related to sampling at hazardous waste sites and to provide a quick reference to websites and documents that can assist field personnel in implementing a site characterization plan. Several recommendations are listed to assist field personnel in developing the skills necessary to oversee or perform hazardous waste sampling.

The Bureau of Land Management

The BLM's National Science and Technology Center (NSTC) provides senior technical services and support to BLM offices in the following areas:

- Evaluation and cleanup of hazardous substance releases
- Cost recovery/cost avoidance associated with the cleanup/restoration and resource injury resulting from releases of hazardous substances
- Air and water quality issues related to the public lands
- Compliance with environmental laws and regulations

NSTC personnel can assist in the development and implementation of a site-specific work plan, provide contracting assistance, or provide technical oversight for field activities. Call NSTC at 303-236-2772 or visit the website at www.blm.gov/nstc for more information.

The BLM's National Training Center (NTC) provides training related to hazardous waste sites and abandoned mine site investigation. Further training is suggested for those personnel new to the field of environmental investigations. Some of the courses include:

- Characterization of Abandoned Mine Lands (1703-14)
- Environmental Site Assessment (1703-13)
- Hazardous Materials Management—The Basics (1703-00)
- Law Enforcement in Environmental Compliance and Pollution Prevention (1703-10)

Call NTC at 602-926-5500 or visit the website at www.ntc.blm.gov.

The Environmental Protection Agency

The EPA's National Service Center for Environmental Publications (NSCEP) maintains and distributes EPA publications in hardcopy, CD ROM, and other multimedia formats. Each month, NSCEP produces a list of new titles available from the Center. There are a number of ways to get this information or to order publications.

- **Internet:** Access at http://www.epa.gov/ncepi-hom.

- **Phone:** Call 1-800-490-9198 or (513) 489-8190. You can speak to an operator Monday through Friday, 7:30 a.m. to 5:30 p.m., EST. You can leave an order 24 hours a day.

- **Fax:** Send your order 24/7 to 513-489-8695

- **Mail:**
  U.S. EPA/NSCEP
  P.O. Box 42419
  Cincinnati, Ohio 45242-0419

There is an electronic list server for people who want to keep current with new EPA publications. To receive the new titles listing by e-mail, access the link provided or send an e-mail with a subject line of "Subscribe to nscepnew@one.net." Subscriptions can also be called in to the toll-free number or e-mailed to nscepnew@one.net with the Subject listed as Subscribe and a note stating that you would like to subscribe to the NSCEP New EPA Publications List Serve. The new titles list can also be accessed at: http://yosemite.epa.gov/ncepihom/nsCatalog.nsf/newpubs?OpenView&Start=1>yosemite.epa.gov/ncepihom.

References

Keith, Lawrence H. 1996. Principles of Environmental Sampling, Second Edition. American Chemical Society. Washington, DC.

Naval Facilities Engineering Command and the U.S. Environmental Protection Agency. 1998. Field Sampling and Analysis Technologies Matrix and Reference Guide, First Edition.

Environmental Protection Agency. 2002. Guidance for Quality Assurance Project Plans, [QA/G-5]. EPA/240/R-02/009. Washington, DC.

Environmental Protection Agency. 2002b. RCRA Waste Sampling Draft Technical Guidance— Planning, Implementation and Assessment. EPA530-D-02-002.

Environmental Protection Agency. 1998. Requirements for Quality Assurance Project Plans [QA/R-5]. Washington, DC.

Environmental Protection Agency. 1996. Engineering Support Branch, Standard Operating Procedures and Quality Assurance Manual. Region IV, Environmental Services Division.

Environmental Protection Agency. 1994. Guidance for the Data Quality Objectives Process [QA/G-4]. EPA/600/R-96/055.

Environmental Protection Agency. 1990. Quality Assurance/Quality Control Guidance for Removal Activities: Sampling QA/QC Plan and Data Validation Procedures. Interim Final. EPA/540/G-90/004.

Weiner, Scott. 1992. Field Sampling Procedures Manual. New Jersey Department of Environmental Protection and Energy.